Wild Stunts

STUNNING
MOTORCYCLE
STUNTS

by Tyler Omoth

Raintree is an imprint of Capstone Global Library Limited, a company incorporated in England and Wales having its registered office at 7 Pilgrim Street, London, EC4V 6LB – Registered company number: 6695582

www.raintree.co.uk
myorders@raintree.co.uk

Edited by Nate LeBoutillier
Designed by Kyle Grenz
Picture research by Jo Miller
Production by Tori Abraham

ISBN 978 1 4747 0617 9
19 18 17 16 15
10 9 8 7 6 5 4 3 2 1

British Library Cataloguing in Publication Data
A full catalogue record for this book is available from the British Library

Acknowledgements
Corbis: Bettmann, 6, Bo Bridges, 21; Courtesy of Ruth Fisher, 8; Denver Post via Getty Images/Hyoung Chang, 23; Getty Images: The LIFE Picture Collection/Ralph Crane, 19; Newscom: Icon SMI/Shelly Castellano, 12-13, imageBROKER/Jacek Bilski, 11, Reuters/India/Stringer, 14-15, ZUMA Press/Gene Blevins, 24-25, ZUMA Press/Martin Philbey, 20; Red Bull via Getty Images: Chris Tedesco, 5, Rich Van Every, 28-29; Rex Features via AP Images, 27; Shutterstock: Christian Bertrand, 16-17, Ivan Garcia, cover; The Image Works: Mirropix, 9, Scherl/SZ Photo, 7; The Kobal Collection: CAROLCO, 26
Design Elements
Shutterstock: antishock, Igorsky, Leigh Prather, Kopirin, Radoman Durkovic
Direct Quotations
Page 14, from July 13, 2009 *ESPN* article "Robbie Maddison jumps Tower Bridge in London," xgames.espn.go.com.
Page 19, from November 20, 2007, *Esquire* article "What I've Learned: Evel Knievel," www.esquire.com.
Page 24, from *The Daily Epic* article "This motorcyclist was paid $2 million to do the craziest stunt of all time," www.thedailyepic.com.
Page 26, from *Entertainment Weekly* article "The art of motorcycle mayhem" by Frank Spotnitz, www.ew.com.

Printed in China.

Contents

Flying into the
record books 4

The early days of
motorcycles and stunts 6

Elements of the
motorcycle stunt 10

Famous stunt men and
stunt women 18

Famous motorcycle stunts 24

Glossary 30
Read more 31
Website 31
Index 32

Flying into the record books

Sitting on your bike in front of a *quarter pipe*, you can see the crowd through your helmet. They cheer and wave banners. You're here to break the record for the highest motorcycle jump ever.

The ramp in front of you rises straight up and is ready to launch you into the air. You double-check your bike and your safety equipment. You need speed to do this correctly. Revving your engine, you ride towards the ramp to do an easy jump. It's perfect. One more for good measure, and then you hit the *accelerator*, pushing your bike to the limit.

You hit the ramp and soar up into the air. You turn the bike down towards the landing ramp and return to ground, landing safely. You've done it! It's a brand new world record. You just jumped higher than anyone has ever jumped before!

quarter pipe ramp with a slightly convex surface, used by motorcyclists to perform jumps and other manoeuvres

accelerator lever, pedal or handle used to control the speed of an engine

5

The early days of motorcycles and stunts

Born to push limits

In 1867, Sylvester H. Roper developed a bicycle-like machine that used steam power. The frame was made of wood, and the wheels were wood and iron. Roper lived in Massachusetts, USA, and demonstrated his new invention up and down the East Coast of the United States at fairs and circuses. In 1885, German inventor Gottlieb Daimler improved upon this design with the first diesel-powered motorcycle. From that point on, motorcycles have continued to improve.

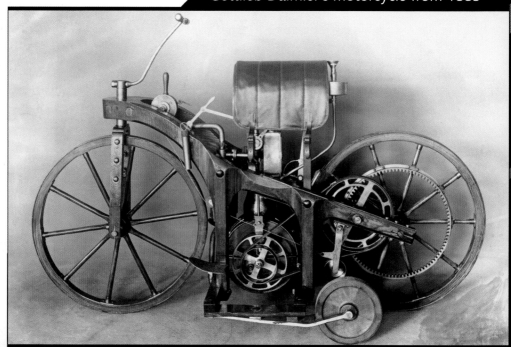
Gottlieb Daimler's motorcycle from 1885

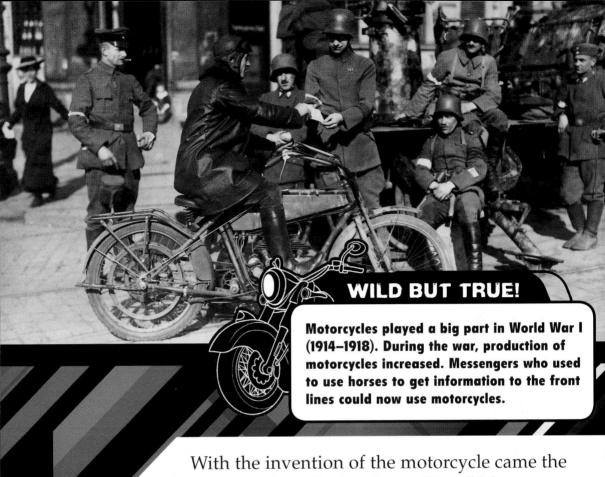

WILD BUT TRUE!

Motorcycles played a big part in World War I (1914–1918). During the war, production of motorcycles increased. Messengers who used to use horses to get information to the front lines could now use motorcycles.

With the invention of the motorcycle came the desire to push its limits. Orren "Putt" Mossman was a *motorcycle stunt man* who bought his first motorcycle in 1926. As he drove it home, he stood on the seat to impress two young ladies. They clapped for him, and an idea was born. He could do motorcycle tricks to make money. Soon Mossman was performing jumps, each bigger than the last. Mossman recruited more riders and formed a *troupe* that travelled the United States performing their stunts.

motorcycle stunt man person who performs special skills involving acrobatic manoeuvring of the bike and sometimes the rider; common manoeuvres include wheelies, stoppies and burnouts

troupe group of motorcyclists or other entertainers who tour different venues to perform an act

Early motorcycle daredevils

Nick DeRush was a film stunt man in the 1930s. When not working on a film, he liked to take his Harley Davidson motorcycle to the pier. There, he would ask people if they'd like to see him ride off of the end of the dock. People loved to watch his unusual performance. Soon Nick and his friends became a travelling motorcycle stunt show.

As early as 1927, a team of horse and motorcycle stunt riders from Yorkshire began demonstrating stunts. The team, known as the White Helmets, still performs today with as many as 30 riders.

Nick DeRush on his motorcycle

The White Helmets display team comprises of men and women serving in the British Royal Corps of Signals. The British Royal Corps of Signals is a branch of the British Army.

People enjoy the daring and unusual tricks that can be performed with motorcycles. Each stunt rider wants to hold a wheelie the longest, jump the highest and ride faster than ever.

Elements of the motorcycle stunt

In the early days of motorcycles, there were few types of motorcycles, so riders would use similar models. Different styles evolved over time. Today, manufacturers make some bikes heavy for long, comfortable rides. Others, called sport bikes, are made for speed and performance. These are the bikes that push the limits of stunts.

Wheelies and *stoppies* require bikes with balance and strong brakes. While most bikes use a foot brake, many stunt bikes also have a hand brake to allow the rider to have better control. Extra brake *calipers* on the wheels help to increase the braking efficiency.

Stunt bikes might have added pegs as a place for riders to place their feet during tricks. Rear seats, *mudguards* and even fuel tanks can be altered. This allows the rider to stand up during a stunt. A 12 o'clock bar can be added to the back of the bike for the bike to rest on while doing a wheelie.

stoppie trick in which the back wheel is lifted and the bike is ridden on the front wheel by carefully applying brake pressure

calipers set of clamps at the end of a brake cable that press against a wheel's rim to stop the wheel from turning

mudguard covering over a motorcycle wheel that protects the wheel against damage

CHECK THIS OUT! Some riders have special mudguards that drag on the ground during wheelies and send sparks shooting into the air.

Bikes that fly

For *aerial* stunts such as jumps and freestyle acrobatics, riders need very light bikes. This allows them to *manoeuvre* in mid-air. Options such as kickstands, electric starters, and headlights are not installed on these bikes in order to keep weight down. Seats are often shaved down to create easier movement for the rider. Rear mudguards are usually removed so they don't interfere with the tricks.

aerial trick that is performed in the air

manoeuvre planned and controlled movement that requires skill

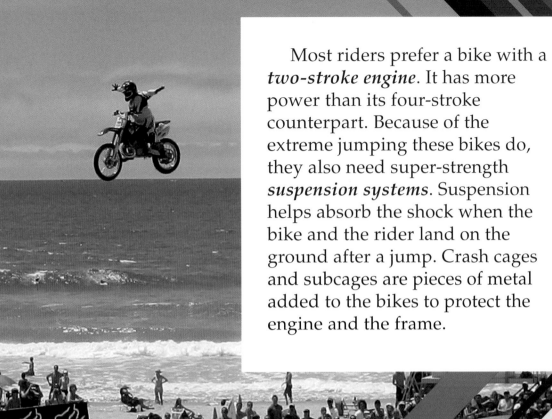

Most riders prefer a bike with a *two-stroke engine*. It has more power than its four-stroke counterpart. Because of the extreme jumping these bikes do, they also need super-strength *suspension systems*. Suspension helps absorb the shock when the bike and the rider land on the ground after a jump. Crash cages and subcages are pieces of metal added to the bikes to protect the engine and the frame.

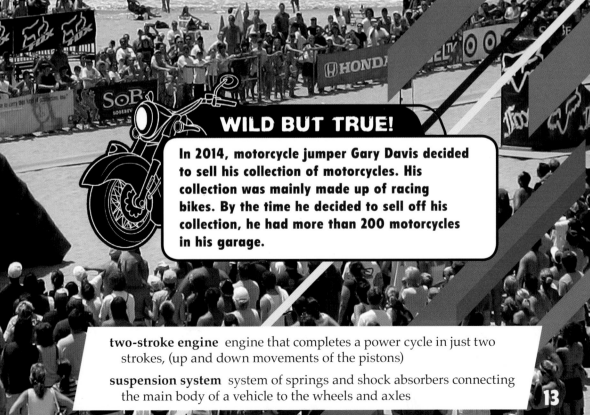

WILD BUT TRUE!

In 2014, motorcycle jumper Gary Davis decided to sell his collection of motorcycles. His collection was mainly made up of racing bikes. By the time he decided to sell off his collection, he had more than 200 motorcycles in his garage.

two-stroke engine engine that completes a power cycle in just two strokes, (up and down movements of the pistons)

suspension system system of springs and shock absorbers connecting the main body of a vehicle to the wheels and axles

The tools of the trade

While many stunts only require the rider and the bike itself, there are many other pieces of equipment that can play a part.

Ramps are essential for jumps. There are many styles of ramp, each designed for a specific jump. Some are for distance while others are shaped to provide height for freestyle tricks. Some riders jump over other things as well. Cars, buses, flaming hoops and even moving trains have all been obstacles for motorcycle jumpers.

CHECK THIS OUT! In 2009, Robbie Maddison used London's Tower Bridge as a ramp. After jumping the gap between drawbridges, Maddison said, "It was an incredible feeling to fly between the two towers and over the Thames".

Some riders use a large metal sphere to ride in circles and even upside down. Sometimes they even put several riders into one sphere creating a dizzying whir of motion.

Stunts that aim for speed records need a precise radar gun to record the speed of the bike. For timed events such as holding a wheelie, officials may use a stopwatch.

Using a ramp, this stunt rider jumps through a flaming hoop

Preparing for the worst

With every motorcycle stunt, there are dangers involved. Proper safety equipment and procedures are crucial to a successful stunt. Riders use helmets to protect their heads in case of a fall. They protect their elbows and knees with extra pads and braces. Fire can be a major hazard in a stunt. Many riders wear special fire suits designed to protect them from heat and flames.

Some jumps require safety nets to catch the rider in case of a fall. Special padded walls provide safe barriers if riders cannot stop their bikes where they land.

Safety equipment is not the only way to keep riders safe. Understanding the necessary speeds and angles for various stunts, will help riders to perform stunts more successfully. It takes professional stunt riders years of training to learn how to master their tricks.

CHECK **THIS** OUT!

Performing wheelies on public roads is illegal in most countries.

Famous stunt men and stunt women

Evel unparalleled

When it comes to motorcycle stunts, one name stands out above the rest: Evel Knievel. Between 1965 and 1980 Knievel attempted more than 75 spectacular jumps. With his fancy leather jumpsuits and cape, he mesmerized crowds with his amazing jumps. He once jumped over 22 parked cars. He also jumped over coaches, pits full of rattlesnakes and even a pool containing 13 sharks!

On New Year's Eve in 1967 he attempted to jump the fountains at Caesar's Palace in Las Vegas, USA, but failed. He was injured in the crash. Knievel suffered 433 broken bones over the course of his career. Knievel's Harley Davidson XR-750 motorcycle is on display at the Smithsonian National Museum of American History in Washington D.C., USA. During his career Knievel championed motorcycle safety – especially the importance of wearing a helmet.

WILD BUT TRUE!

Evel Knievel's son, Robbie, followed in his father's footsteps as a stunt rider. At the age of four he was jumping his bicycle. By the age of seven he was riding a motorcycle. In 1989, Robbie successfully jumped the fountains at Caesar's Palace in honour of his father.

"Anybody can jump a motorcycle. The trouble begins when you try to land it."
Evel Knievel

The best on bikes

When a great rider lands a new stunt, there is always a desire to do something bigger and better. Today's top stunt riders compete with each other to pull off the most insane tricks.

Robbie "Maddo" Maddison is an Australian rider who loves to push the limits. He's set world records for the longest ramp jump several times and was even a *stunt double* for James Bond in *Skyfall*.

Carey Hart invented a trick called the Hart Attack. It's where a rider puts one hand on the seat and the other hand on the handlebar and does a handstand. All in mid-air!

Carey Hart performs the Hart Attack

stunt double person who takes the place of an actress or actor in an action scene or when a special skill or great risk is called for

Travis Pastrana performs a double backflip

The X Games in the United States is one of the premier stages for freestyle stunt riders. Travis Pastrana was the first to land a double backflip in competition at the X Games. He won his first X Games gold medal at the age of 15. Mike Metzger, another X Games champion, once did a motorcycle backflip over the fountains at Caesar's Palace. Brian Deegan has tallied more X Games medals than any other rider. In 2014, he had accumulated 13 medals.

CHECK THIS OUT!

Freestyle was not considered an official sport for many years. In 1998, the Freestyle Motocross Association was created to establish rules for the sport.

Daring women

Motorcycle stunt riding is not just for men. Many women excel at stunt riding. In 1939, Theresa Wallach became the first woman to receive the British Motorcycle Racing Club's Gold Star. She received the award for averaging more than 161 kilometres (100 miles) per hour on the famous Brooklands circuit in Surrey. Bessie "BB" Stringfield performed hill-climbing stunts and trick riding in live stunt shows across the United States. She even served as a motorcycle dispatch rider during World War II (1939–1945).

Today, even more women are involved in motorcycle stunt riding. At just 18 years old, Debbie Evans jumped a motorcycle over a 9-metre (30-foot) ravine for a film scene. That stunt sparked a Hall of Fame career performing both car and motorcycle stunts for films. At just 1.56-metres (5-ft 2-in) tall and weighing just 51 kilograms (8 stone), Jessica Maine is known as "Smallz". Maine is a pioneer of women's wheelies competitions and exhibitions.

CHECK THIS OUT!

Ashley Fiolek is a deaf stunt rider who performs in Marvel's Universe Live Show. She learned to ride in the woods at her grandfather's cabin in Michigan, USA.

Ashley Fiolek

Famous motorcycle stunts

Some stunts are impressive. Others are so wild and imaginative that they become legendary.

Ten-storey drop

On New Year's Eve in 2008, Robbie Maddison jumped from a ramp to the top of a 10-storey building in Las Vegas, USA. From there he proceeded to ride off of the roof to land safely on another ramp.

"Even if you paid me $10 million, I'd never do it again."

Robbie Maddison, on his "Ten-Storey Drop" stunt.

Grand Canyon jump

Robbie Knievel jumped over a portion of the Grand Canyon, clearing 69 metres (228 ft). The canyon at the jump site was 762- metres (2,500-ft) deep. He crashed and broke his leg on the landing.

Great Wall jump

In 1993, Eddie Kidd jumped his motorcycle over the Great Wall of China. Kidd performed motorcycle stunts in many films, including the 1981 film *Riding High*.

WILD BUT TRUE!

In 1975, "Super" Joe Einhorn vowed to jump Niagara Falls on a rocket-powered motorcycle. However, he suffered a head injury during a jump at *Santa Fe Speedway* in Illinois, USA, which meant he was unable to attempt the Niagara Falls jump.

Jumping out of the big screen

Motorcycle stunts are always memorable scenes on the big screen. Here are some of the most amazing movie stunts performed on two wheels.

Terminator 2 – Stunt man Bob Brown, as "T-1000," took a 58-metre (190-ft) run-up to crash his Kawasaki 650 through a window. Brown flew through broken glass before a safety cable caught him and lowered him onto a safety pad.

Bob Brown crashes through a window in *Terminator 2*

"It's like your body is saying, 'Get me out of here!' But you've got to tell yourself, 'I'm going to go through that window, and nobody's going to see me blink'."
Bob Brown, on his jump in the film *Terminator 2*

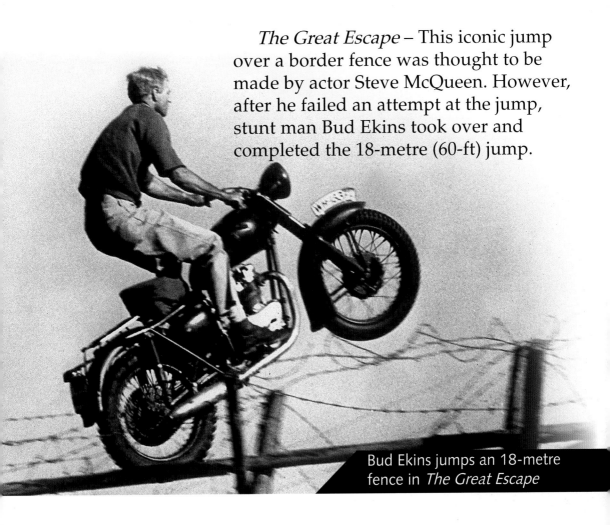

The Great Escape – This iconic jump over a border fence was thought to be made by actor Steve McQueen. However, after he failed an attempt at the jump, stunt man Bud Ekins took over and completed the 18-metre (60-ft) jump.

Bud Ekins jumps an 18-metre fence in *The Great Escape*

Tomorrow Never Dies – In a dramatic chase scene, James Bond escapes a pursuing helicopter on a BMW motorcycle. Stunt man Jean Pierre also had a passenger sitting across his lap. The exciting scene took three weeks to film and finished with a motorcycle jump over the helicopter.

WILD BUT TRUE!

Stunt innovator Dar Robinson didn't break a single bone in his 19-year Hollywood career. Tragically, he was killed while filming a routine high-speed chase scene on the set of *Million Dollar Mystery* on 21 November 1986.

Jumping, speeding and popping into the record books

Motorcycle stunts are highly competitive. The best riders end up in the record books.

Highest jump

On 25 July 2009 Ronnie Renner blasted off of a quarter pipe to a height of 19.3 metres (over 63 ft) above the ground. His jump topped his own record of 18.2 metres (nearly 60 ft).

WORLD RECORDS

CERTIFICATE

The record for the highest air on a motorcycle quarterpipe jump was achieved by Ronnie Renner (USA) during Red Bull High Rise in Grant Park at Butler Field in Chicago, Illinois, USA on 25 July 2009

GUINNESS WORLD RECORDS LTD

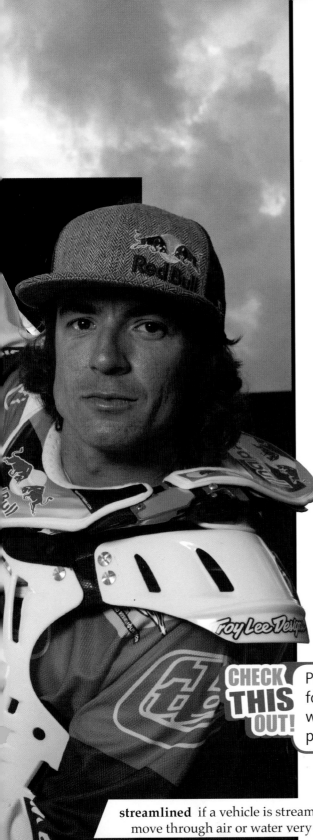

Longest ramp jump

Ryan Capes sailed with his bike through the air for an astounding 119 metres (390 ft). That's the length of a football pitch.

Wheelie

Riding a wheelie for a couple of metres is dangerous enough. Japanese rider Yasuyuki Kudo rode his bike with one wheel up for an amazing 331 kilometres (205.7 miles). That's an amazing feat of balance and strength.

Fastest motorcycle

Rocky Robinson drove a specially *streamlined* motorcycle to break the world record with a speed of 376 miles (605 km) per hour. Aeroplanes cruise at 575 miles (925 km) per hour.

CHECK THIS OUT!

Patrick Furstenhoff holds the record for the highest speed reached on one wheel with his 191.3 mile (307.9 km) per hour wheelie.

streamlined if a vehicle is streamlined, it is designed so that it can move through air or water very quickly and easily

Glossary

accelerator lever, pedal or handle used to control the speed of an engine

aerial trick that is performed in the air

calipers set of clamps at the end of a brake cable that press against a wheel's rim to stop the wheel from turning

manoeuvre planned and controlled movement that requires skill

motorcycle stunt man person who performs special skills involving acrobatic manoeuvring of the bike and sometimes the rider; common manoeuvres include wheelies, stoppies and burnouts

mudguard covering over a motorcycle wheel that protects the wheel against damage

quarter pipe ramp with a slightly convex surface, used by motorcyclists to perform jumps and other manoeuvres

stoppie trick in which the back wheel is lifted and the bike is ridden on the front wheel by carefully applying brake pressure

streamlined if a vehicle is streamlined, it is designed so that it can move through air or water very quickly and easily

stunt double person who takes the place of an actress or actor in an action scene or when a special skill or great risk is called for

suspension system system of springs and shock absorbers connecting the main body of a vehicle to the wheels and axles

troupe group of motorcyclists or other entertainers who tour different venues to perform an act

two-stroke engine engine that completes a power cycle in just two strokes, (up and down movements of the pistons)

Read more

Extreme Athletes (Ultimate Adventurers),
Charlotte Guillain (Raintree, 2014)

Motor Sports (Fantastic Sport Facts), Michael Hurley
(Raintree, 2014)

Race that Bike! Forces in Vehicles (Feel the Force),
Angela Royston (Raintree, 2015)

Wheel Sports (Extreme Sport), Michael Hurley
(Raintree, 2013)

Website

www.guinnessworldrecords.com
Search the Guinness World Records website for
astounding motorcycle stunts and records, including the
fastest motorcycle wheelie on ice, the heaviest rideable
motorcycle and the most number of people on
a motorcycle!

Index

Brown, Bob 26

Capes, Ryan 29

Daimler, Gottlieb 6
Davis, Gary 13
Deegan, Brian 21
DeRush, Nick 8

Ekins, Bud 27
Einhorn, Joe 25
Evans, Debbie 22

Fiolek, Ashley 22, 23

Harley Davidson motorcycles 8, 18
"Hart Attack" 20
Hart, Carey 20

Kidd, Eddie 25
Knievel, Evel 18, 19
Knievel, Robbie 18, 25
Kudo, Yasuyuki 29

Maddison, Robbie "Maddo" 14, 20, 24
Maine, Jessica "Smallz" 22
McQueen, Steve 27
Metzger, Mike 21
Mossman, Orren "Putt" 7

Pastrana, Travis 21
Pierre, Jean 27

Renner, Ronnie 28
Robinson, Dar 27
Robinson, Rocky 29
Roper, Sylvester H. 6

safety equipment 4, 16, 17, 18, 26
stoppies 10
Stringfield, Bessie "BB" 22

The White Helmets 8, 9

Wallach, Theresa 22
wheelies 9, 10, 11, 15, 17, 22, 29

X Games 21